Empires in the Middle Ages

The Mongol Empire

Edited by
Carolyn DeCarlo

Britannica®
Educational Publishing
in association with
ROSEN
Educational Services

Published in 2018 by Britannica Educational Publishing (a trademark of Encyclopædia Britannica, Inc.) in association with The Rosen Publishing Group, Inc., 29 East 21st Street, New York, NY 10010

Distributed exclusively by Rosen Publishing.
To see additional Britannica Educational Publishing titles, go to rosenpublishing.com.

First Edition

Britannica Educational Publishing
J.E. Luebering: Executive Director, Core Editorial
Andrea R. Field: Managing Editor, Compton's by Britannica

Rosen Publishing
Carolyn DeCarlo: Editor
Nelson Sá: Art Director
Brian Garvey: Designer
Cindy Reiman: Photography Manager
Nicole DiMella: Photo Researcher

Library of Congress Cataloging-in-Publication Data

Names: DeCarlo, Carolyn, editor.
Title: The Mongol Empire / edited by Carolyn DeCarlo.
Description: New York : Britannica Educational Publishing, in Association with Rosen Educational Services, 2018. | Series: Empires in the Middle Ages | Includes bibliographical references and index. | Audience: Grades 5–8.
Identifiers: LCCN 2017021126| ISBN 9781680487848 (library bound : alk. paper) | ISBN 9781680488661 (pbk. : alk. paper) | ISBN 9781680488678 (6 pack : alk. paper)
Subjects: LCSH: Mongols—History—Juvenile literature.
Classification: LCC DS19 .D456 2018 | DDC 950/.2—dc23
LC record available at https://lccn.loc.gov/2017021126

Manufactured in the United States of America

Photo credits: Cover Universal History Archive/Universal Images Group/Getty Images; p. 4 © Paolo Koch-Rapho/Photo Researchers; pp. 5, 14 © George Holton/Photo Researchers; pp. 6, 29, 40 © Encyclopædia Britannica, Inc.; pp. 9, 17, 37 © Courtesy of the National Palace Museum, Taipei, Taiwan, Republic of China; p. 10 © Courtesy of the Edinburgh University Library, Scotland; p. 12 Pictures from History/Bridgeman Images; p. 18 © Susan Pierres/Peter Arnold, Inc.; p. 20 © The Nelson-Atkins Museum of Art, Kansas City, Missouri; purchase Nelson Trust (72-8); p. 22 © Photos.com/Jupiterimages; p. 25 © Jonathan Wright/Bruce Coleman Inc.; p. 27 Heritage Images/Hulton Archive/Getty Images; p. 30 Karasev Victor/Shutterstock.com; p. 31 © Courtesy of the Trustees of the British Museum; photograph, J.R. Freeman & Co. Ltd.; p. 35 © Jupiterimages-Photos.com/Thinkstock; p. 39 © Robert Smith.

CONTENTS

INTRODUCTION

The traditional homeland of the Central Asian people known as the Mongols is a vast highland region called the Mongolian Plateau, which is now divided politically into the independent country of Mongolia (historically called Outer Mongolia) and an autonomous region of China (Inner Mongolia). The Mongols share a common language and a tradition of following a nomadic way of life herding livestock. They also share a most remarkable history. The Mongol Empire, which began in the early thirteenth century CE,

Horses graze on the steppes in the southern region of the Gobi, a desert straddling the China-Mongolia border. The Altai Mountains can be seen in the distance beyond the desert's western reaches.

was formed when various nomadic Mongol tribes came together in a single nation, and it expanded to become one of the greatest continental empires of all time.

A woman cares for her goats outside a tent-like dwelling known as a yurt in part of the Gobi Desert. A traditional lifestyle in Mongolia today is not so different from what it would have been during the Mongol Empire.

Over many centuries, including the period of the Mongol Empire, the social structure and culture of the Mongols showed very little change. Traditional Mongol society was based on the family, the clan, and the tribe, with clan names derived from those of common male ancestors. As clans merged, the tribal name was taken from that of the strongest clan. In the tribe, weaker clans retained their own headmen and livestock but were subordinate to the strongest clan. In periods of tribal unity, khans (Mongol monarchs) assigned commanders to territories from which troops and revenues were gathered. Mongol history alternated between periods of tribal conflict and tribal consolidation.

Among the tribes that held power in Mongolia were the Xiongnu, a confederated empire that warred with the young Chinese state for centuries before dissolving in 48 CE. The Khitan ruled in Manchuria and North China, where they established the Liao dynasty (907–1125) and formed an alliance with a little-known tribal confederacy known as All the Mongols. After the fall of the Liao, the Tatars—a Mongol people but not members of the league—appeared as allies of the Juchen, the Khitan's successors.

During this time, Genghis Khan came to power within the All the Mongols league and was proclaimed

The Mongol Empire grew to cover a vast territory.

khan in 1206. He skillfully gained control over the Mongols outside the league. Under the leadership of Genghis Khan and his successors, the Mongols established an empire that reached from what are now China and Korea in the east to eastern Europe and the shores of the Persian Gulf in the west. At the height of their power, they overthrew the rulers of northern and southern China and reunited China under Mongol rule, as the Yuan dynasty. The Mongols were the first foreigners to rule all of China. The western part of their empire, in Russia and eastern Europe, was known as the Golden Horde. The power of the Mongol Empire declined greatly in the fourteenth century.

CHAPTER 1

GENGHIS KHAN AND HIS SUCCESSORS

In 1206, Genghis Khan was elected head of the All the Mongols league, a confederation of Mongol tribes, and founded the Mongol dynasty. Between 1206 and 1227, when Genghis Khan died, the Mongols conquered a dominion that stretched from the China Sea to the Caspian. On the north, it bordered the forest belt of Siberia, and on the south it touched the Kunlun Mountains, Tibet, and the central plains of China. The Mongols' impressive military conquests were largely due to their armies of archers mounted on horseback, who possessed great speed and mobility.

CALCULATED ADVANCES

The first attack by the Mongols under Genghis Khan was launched against the Xi Xia, who occupied a border state in northwestern China. They next began to fight the Jin dynasty, which controlled the rest of northern

Genghis Khan is depicted in ink on silk in a painting in the National Palace Museum in Taipei, Taiwan.

China. By 1215, the Mongols had taken the Jin capital of Yanjing (now Beijing). They eventually conquered all of northern China. By 1225, they had taken Turkistan, in Central Asia. Advance troops penetrated into southern Russia and raided cities in Crimea.

The Mongol Empire created by Genghis Khan was not a unified state but a vast collection of territories held together by military force. Because it was controlled by so many military leaders, all theoretically responsible to a leader known as the great

MONGOL WARRIORS

A Mongol warrior did not join the army but, rather, was born into it. Every Mongol man who could ride a horse was a soldier, and all became expert equestrians. Mongol children were put on horseback and instructed in archery from a very young age. The Mongol warrior was always ready to fight, whether he was hunting wild animals or going to war. He met both challenges with vigor and an eagerness to prove his courage and fighting expertise.

Because Mongols fought on horseback, their weapons were usually designed to be used while riding. The most prized was the bow. Mongol warriors might take up to a year making a bow and usually carried several into battle. A warrior carried as many as sixty arrows. Different kinds of arrows were used for different situations. Some were best for long distances. Others were suitable for piercing armor or injecting poison into a victim. Mongols also carried lances, maces, daggers, and curved swords called sabers.

This miniature painting of Mongol warriors was created for an Islamic history book from 1307, Rashid al-Din's *History of the World.*

Mongol leather armor protected both the

warrior and his horse. Later, many soldiers wore iron scales or chain mail. A Mongol warrior cared for his own weapons, equipment, food, and up to five extra horses. Discipline in caring for these items was imperative: even commanding officers could be punished for ill-equipped soldiers.

The Mongols were not always the army with the best weapons, the strongest armor, or the largest forces, yet they were often the victors. Unparalleled ferocity, dazzling battlefield tactics, and brilliant leadership were common factors in their successes. Extraordinary discipline was also an essential component; in fact, desertion meant death.

khan, the empire carried within it the seeds of its own breakdown.

Central power rested with the great khan and his councillors. Although they were well organized militarily, the Mongols had no developed concept for ruling settled populations. The various territories were placed under the authority of military commanders. Most new conquests were not governed—just economically exploited. In areas that were under prolonged subjugation, there was some growth of administration. Local bureaucracies, though dominated by Mongols, usually followed administrative patterns that had been locally developed. This was especially true in China, with its ancient and vast bureaucracy.

THE SECRET HISTORY OF THE MONGOLS

A significant work of early Mongolian literature relates the details of the Mongols' rise. *Mongqolun niuča tobča'an*, or the *Secret History of the Mongols*, is a chronicle of the deeds of Genghis Khan and of his son Ogodei, written no earlier than 1228 CE and recorded partly in praise of the two leaders, partly to preserve that era of history.

Ogodei Khan was the second great khan of the Mongol Empire, succeeding his father.

Much of what we know about Genghis Khan's legendary life comes from the embellished *Secret History of the Mongols*. Several stories illustrate his power of attracting supporters through sheer force of personality, even as a young man. According to one story, he was captured by the Taychiut, a rival clan. Rather than killing him, the Taychiut fastened a wooden collar around his neck and kept him around their camps. One night while they were feasting, Genghis Khan knocked down the sentry with a blow and fled. The Taychiut searched for him all night. When he was finally found, the man who discovered him—impressed by the fire in his eyes—helped him escape at the risk of his own life.

Just how much any of these stories are true and how much has been fictionalized remains a mystery, but what they do reveal for certain is how great a figure Genghis Khan was, even in his own time.

DIVISION BETWEEN SONS

While Genghis Khan was still living, he divided the empire between his four sons by his favorite wife. Tolui, the youngest, received eastern Mongolia. Ogodei received western Mongolia and part of northwestern China. Chagatai was given most of Turkistan and part of western China. The oldest son, Jochi, received southwestern Siberia, western Turkistan, and the Russian lands stretching north of the Black Sea.

Genghis Khan and Jochi both died in 1227. At a convocation of Mongol leaders, Ogodei was appointed great khan. Ogodei made his capital at Karakorum in central Mongolia. He immediately set out to add more

An ancient stone tortoise stands in front of the monastery of Erdeni Dzu. Erdeni Dzu was built in 1585 on the ruins of of Karakorum, Mongolia. The city was once an early center for sculpture and was especially note-worthy for its great stone tortoises.

of China to the Mongol empire, dominating his brothers and undertaking further conquests. Jochi's lands in the west were inherited by his son, Batu, who seized control of Russia and terrorized eastern Europe. In the east, advances were made into China. By 1234, all but the southernmost region of China had been incorporated.

With Ogodei's death in 1241, the branches fell into intrigue and war among themselves for leadership. Guyuk, a son of Ogodei's widow, was elected great khan in 1246 but died two years later. He was succeeded by Mongke, a son of Tolui, who became great khan in 1248 and continued an expansionist policy. Under him, the empire was expanded into unsubdued neighboring countries. The main new conquest was in the Middle East. Hulegu, a brother of Mongke, conquered what are now Iran, Iraq, and Syria in the 1250s. The only defeat the Mongols suffered was at the hands of the Mamluk dynasty of Egypt in 1260. Hulegu's conquests resulted in the creation of a kingdom of nearly independent rulers, the Il-Khanate dynasty of Persia (present-day Iran).

Mongke's brother Kublai became great khan in 1260, and Mongol power reached its zenith during his rule. The Mongols destroyed the Southern Song dynasty and reunified China under the Yuan, or Mongol, dynasty (1206–1368).

CHAPTER 2

THE YUAN DYNASTY

After Genghis Khan took control of northern China in the early thirteenth century, the Mongols turned their attention to southern China. The final consolidation came under the rule of Kublai, the fifth "great khan" and grandson of Genghis Khan. The reign of Kublai Khan marked a turning point in Mongol history. In theory, he was the ruler of the whole empire, but he came to regard himself primarily as a Chinese emperor. The other parts of the empire began to go their separate ways.

A NEW SEAT OF POWER

Under Kublai, the center of power moved away from Mongolia into China. In 1267, the Mongols moved their capital from Karakorum to Beijing. They built their new capital, Dadu, just outside the old Jin capital, at what is now Beijing. In 1271, Kublai declared himself emperor of China and renamed the dynasty Yuan (meaning "beginning"), to indicate that this was the beginning of a long period of Mongol rule.

The Mongols continued their assault on the Southern Song dynasty. While the Song ruling class and the imperial court were indulging themselves in art and luxurious living in the urban centers, the nomad empire had been on the rise in the north. The formidable Mongol armies, conquerors of Eurasia as far west as eastern Europe and as far east as Korea, finally descended on the Southern Song. Kublai Khan completed the conquest of China in 1279 by conquering the Song dynasty.

Kublai Khan was the grandson of the great Mongol conqueror Genghis Khan. He was the fifth "great khan" of the Mongol Empire and emperor of China in the Yuan, or Mongol, dynasty.

CHANGES FOR CHINA

In China, the Yuan dynasty rebuilt the Grand Canal (the world's longest man-made waterway and one of the great engineering feats of ancient China), put the roads and postal service in good order, and made paper money the sole legal currency throughout China. The Mongol rulers were tolerant about the religious practices of the Chinese. The Mongols also made use of some aspects of Confucian order during their rule. In the Yuan period, many foreigners traveled to China, and many Chinese journeyed to Iran, Russia, and even western Europe.

Cargo barges move in single file along the Grand Canal at Suzhou, China.

However, the Chinese resented their Mongol conquerors. The Mongols kept their own language and customs, rather than adopting Chinese ones, and they barred the Chinese from holding the higher political offices. In fact, the Mongols became the most hated of the barbarian rulers because they did not allow the Chinese ruling class to govern. Instead, they gave the task of governing to foreigners. Distrusting the Chinese, the Mongol rulers placed the southern Chinese at the lowest level of the four classes they created. The extent of this distrust was reflected in their provincial administration. As conquerors, they made the provincial governments into direct extensions of the central chancellery. This practice was continued by succeeding dynasties, resulting in a further concentration of power in the central imperial government.

CONQUEST AND TRADE

Across Asia, Kublai Khan continued his grandfather's dream of world conquest. Two unsuccessful naval expeditions were launched against Japan in 1274 and 1281. Four land expeditions were sent against Dai Viet (now Vietnam) and five against Burma (now Myanmar). However, the Mongol conquests overseas and in Southeast Asia were neither spectacular nor long enduring.

Under the Mongols, China's trade and contacts with foreign countries were more extensive than at any other time before the modern period. The Mongols eliminated state trade controls that had existed under the Song and Jin dynasties. As a result, trade grew to new levels both within China and with other countries. Silk, the major Chinese export, reached the

A detail from the hand scroll *Nine Horses* by Ren Renfa, consisting of ink and colors on silk, dates to c. 1324 during the Yuan dynasty. Silks and ceramics made their way west from China along caravan routes to trading posts in the Middle East during this period.

Middle East and even Europe via the caravan routes across Asia. Chinese ceramics also were exported, chiefly to the Islamic countries of the Middle East. China's trade with the Middle East and Europe, however, was handled by non-Chinese—mainly Persians, Arabs, and Syrians—while direct trade with Europe was concentrated largely within the Italian republics. As a result of foreign contacts, Islamic advances in science and technology were introduced into China. Chinese influences, including in medicine, art, and government, spread to the Middle East and Central Asia.

FALL OF THE DYNASTY

After Kublai Khan's death in 1294 the Mongol Empire fragmented. From 1300 on, disputes over succession weakened the central government in China, and there were frequent rebellions there. Secret societies became increasingly active among the Chinese, and a movement known as the Red Turbans spread throughout the north during the 1350s. In 1356 a rebel leader named Zhu Yuanzhang and his peasant army

WESTERN VIEWS OF THE MONGOLS

The Mongols were regarded with mixed feelings in the West. Although Westerners dreaded the Mongols, the Crusaders hoped to use them in their fight against the Muslims and attempted to negotiate an alliance with them for this purpose. Friar John of Carpini and William of Rubruck were two of the better known Christian missionaries sent to establish these negotiations with the Mongol ruler.

The best Western account of the Mongols was left by a Venetian merchant, Marco Polo, in his *Travels of Marco Polo*. It tells of Polo's travels over the long and perilous land route to China and his experience as a trusted official of Kublai Khan. Kublai reportedly sent Polo on many fact-finding missions to far places in the empire, including Hangzhou in the southeast, Yunnan in the

(Continued on the next page)

(Continued from the previous page)

Marco Polo, his uncle, and his father present the pope's letter to the court of Kublai Khan in this detail from an illuminated manuscript.

southwest, and perhaps also what is now Myanmar (Burma), and from these lands Polo brought back stories of the people and their lives. He may also have had other official responsibilities. Dictated in the early fourteenth century, Polo's book was translated into many languages. Although much of medieval Europe did not believe Polo's tales, some, such as Christopher Columbus, were influenced by Polo's description of the riches of the East.

captured the old capital of Nanjing, on the lower Yangtze River. Within a decade he had won control of the economically important middle and lower reaches of the Yangtze, driving the Mongols to the north. In 1368 he declared himself the emperor, thereby founding the Ming dynasty, and established his capital at Nanjing. Later the same year he captured the Yuan capital of Dadu. The Mongol emperor Shundi fled to Inner Mongolia, and, although Mongol power was not immediately destroyed, historically the Yuan dynasty now came to an end. The rest of China eventually fell easily to Ming troops.

CHAPTER 3

THE GOLDEN HORDE

The western part of the Mongol Empire, referred to as the Golden Horde, flourished from the mid-thirteenth century to the end of the fourteenth century. The people of the Golden Horde were a mixture of Turks and Mongols, with the latter generally constituting the aristocracy.

MONGOLS IN RUSSIA

A series of military campaigns into Russia and eastern Europe was launched by Genghis Khan's grandson, Batu, in 1236. This was the beginning of the Golden Horde. Between 1238 and 1240, the East Slavic state of Kievan Rus was crushed by the onslaught of the Mongols under Batu's leadership. The once-flourishing populace there either perished or fled into the neighboring forests. Resistance in Russia ceased after the fall of Kiev in 1240.

A fisherman prepares his nets to catch beluga sturgeon on the Volga River near Volgograd, Russia. To the east along the Volga, the Mongols once held court at Sarai Berke, one of the capitals of the Golden Horde.

Stunning eastern Europe, Batu's armies reached central Germany before turning southward to establish themselves in Hungary by 1241. The death of Ogodei in 1241 halted the Mongol advance into western Europe. Because the Mongol succession was disputed for several years, Europe was saved from further westward invasion.

The Golden Horde, at its peak, had conquered most of European Russia from the Urals to the Carpathian Mountains, and it extended eastward deep into the steppes of Siberia. The Mongols formed a kingdom with their capital at Sarai Batu on a tributary of the Volga River. The capital was later moved upstream to Sarai Berke, which at its peak held perhaps six hundred thousand inhabitants.

CONTINUING TRADITIONS, NEW TRADE ROUTES

The influence of the Golden Horde was felt to some extent almost everywhere in Russia. Asian customs became a part of Russian culture, but as long as the Russians made tributes (financial payments) demanded by the Mongols, they were free to practice their religion and native customs. The one principality that escaped Mongol domination was Novgorod in the north. Novgorod joined up with the Hanseatic League, a European trading confederation, and flourished.

The Mongols aimed to revive, under a unified political system, the trade that had traditionally crossed the Central Asian steppes and vitalized the economy of the pastoral nomads. As they moved westward, they gained the collaboration of groups of Turkic nomads and the predominantly Iranian and Muslim traders in the towns of the old Silk Road; they encountered the greatest resistance in sedentary political centers and among landowning elites. The lands of the Rus presented numerous similarities with the Central Asian areas that the Mongols had already conquered. There, too, a former commercial empire had fallen apart into an aggregation of warring principalities. Ready recruits were to be found—in the Polovtsians, who controlled the lower Dnieper and Volga and Don, and in the Muslim merchants, who dealt in the towns on the Crimean Peninsula and the upper Volga.

CULTURAL LIFE AND THE "MONGOL INFLUENCE"

Notions that the Mongol invasion destroyed traditional Russian culture and that the period led to isolation from the West do not fit the evidence and should largely be dismissed.

A quarrel between Russian princes before the khan's ambassador in 1296 is depicted by artist Boris Chorikov in the *Illustrated Karamzin.*

In the areas of religion and intellectual life, Asian influence was practically nonexistent. Control of formal culture by the Russian Orthodox and Muslim clergy and limited contact between the Slavic and Turkic populations prevented it. Concerning the secular culture of the court and counting house, however, the situation was different. These spheres were controlled by very pragmatic princes, merchants, and diplomats. There, Slavs and Mongols developed an

(Continued on the next page)

(Continued from the previous page)

international subculture whose language was Turkic and whose administrative techniques were essentially those of the Golden Horde. Slavic merchants took full part in this culture, and Russian princes in particular developed their court and chancellery practices within its context.

Many of the conquered cities adjusted to the new situation. New centers like Muscovy (Moscow) and Tver, hardly mentioned in any source before the Mongol period, arose and flourished in Mongol times. The Mongol invasion was not a catastrophe for everyone. The local princely dynasties continued unchanged in their traditional seats. Few Mongols remained west of the Urals after the conquest; political and fiscal administration was entrusted to the same Turkic clan leaders and Islamic merchants who had for generations operated in the area.

In this way, the Horde was gradually Turkified and Islamized, especially under their greatest khan, Oz Beg. The Turkic tribes concentrated on animal husbandry in the steppes, while their subject peoples—East Slavs, Mordvinians, Greeks, Georgians, and Armenians—contributed tribute. The Russian princes, particularly those of Muscovy, soon obtained responsibility for collecting the local tribute. The Horde carried on an extensive trade with Mediter-

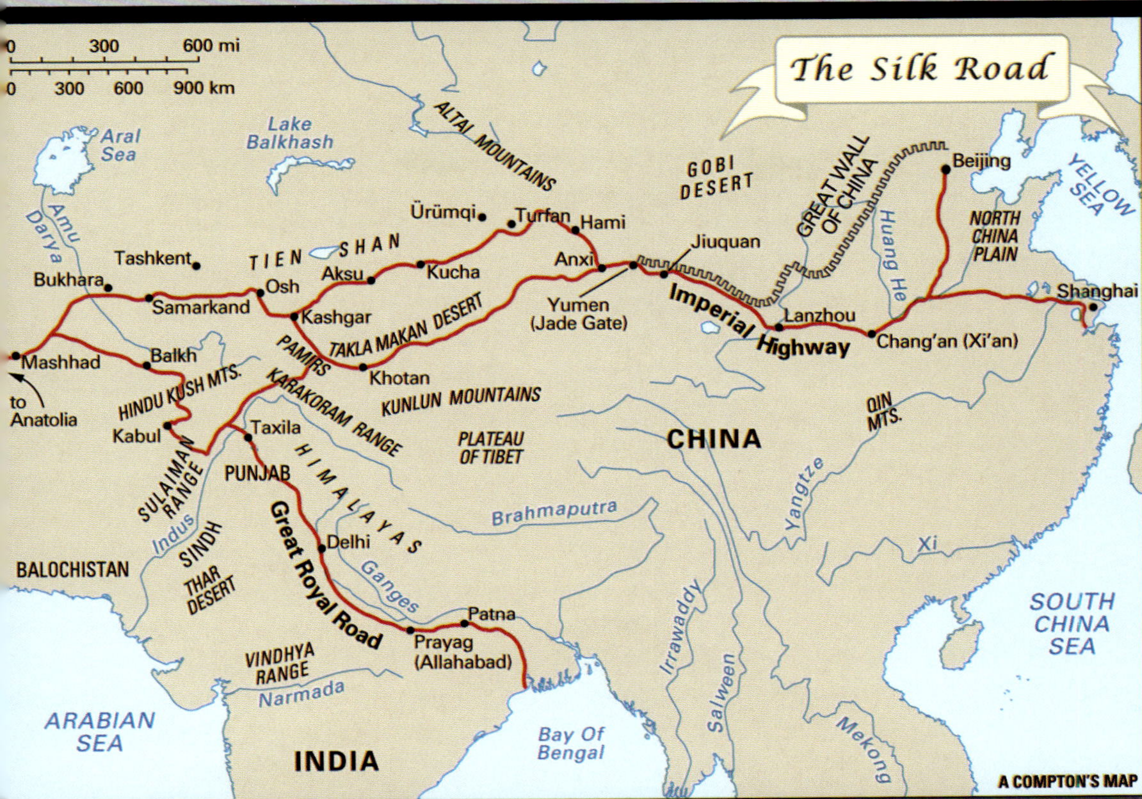

The Silk Road was an ancient trade route linking China with the West that carried goods and ideas between Rome and China. Revived by the Mongols in the thirteenth and fourteenth centuries, the route was used by Western travelers such as Marco Polo.

ranean peoples, particularly their allies in Mamluk Egypt and the Genoese.

THE PLAGUE AND THE PRINCIPALITY

The Black Death, which struck in 1346–47, and the murder of Oz Beg's successor marked the beginning of the Golden Horde's decline. The Russian princes won a signal victory

The Ozbek Han Mosque, the oldest mosque in Crimea, was built in 1314 during the reign of the khan, Oz Beg.

Ivan III, also known as Ivan the Great, played a crucial role in the decline of the Golden Horde and the Mongols' influence in Russia after he stopped paying tribute to the empire.

over the Horde general Mamai at the Battle of Kulikovo in 1380. Mamai's successor and rival, Tokhtamysh, sacked and burned Moscow in retaliation in 1382 and reestablished the Horde's dominion over the Russians. Tokhtamysh had his own power broken, however, by his former ally Timur Lenk, who invaded the Horde's territory in 1395, destroyed Sarai Berke, and deported most of the region's skilled craftsmen to Central Asia, thus depriving the Horde of its technological edge over resurgent Muscovy.

The principality of Muscovy, nestled deep in the forest at the hub of all the major trade routes, developed further as a result of the Mongols' decline in power. Muscovite princes, who efficiently collected the tribute demanded by the Mongols, enhanced their coffers through reward and fraud. Ivan the Great, grand prince of Muscovy, finally stopped paying tribute to the Mongols. The Mongols sent an army against him, but the army withdrew without a battle. Ivan added Novgorod to his domains in 1478 and eventually spread Muscovy's rule to the Arctic. By 1480, Russia was free of serious Mongol threats.

CHAPTER 4

AN EMPIRE IN DECLINE

Throughout the history of the empire, most of the Mongol khans showed little ability at governing. More often than not, they found themselves reliant on their subjects and on foreigners to administer their empire. Over time, power shifted from the Mongols to their bureaucrats. This, in addition to continual feuding among the different khanates, led to the empire's decline.

By 1368 the Mongols had lost China to the native Ming dynasty. In the same period, the Il-Khanate dynasty of Persia disintegrated, and the western Golden Horde eventually broke apart into several smaller khanates, the most important being those of Crimea, Astrakhan, and Kazan. The last notable Mongol conqueror to appear was Timur Lenk, or Tamerlane, who died in 1405. His conquests ranged from India and Russia to the Mediterranean Sea. But Timur's empire was gone by 1506. Finally, the vast Mongol Empire was reduced to the original Mongol homeland and scattered khanates, while Chinese invasions of the homeland shattered Mongol unity.

THE LAST OF THE MONGOL CONQUERORS

In the late fourteenth century, the conqueror Timur Lenk proclaimed himself the restorer of the Mongol Empire. While the name Timur Lenk means "Timur the lame," his handicap did not stop Timur from becoming one of the fiercest and most successful of the conquerors to come out of Central Asia. For almost four decades—from the 1360s until his death—he and his nomad warriors conquered every territory from Mongolia in the east to the Mediterranean lands in the west. The desolation caused by his campaigns gave rise to many legends.

Timur was born near the city of Samarkand (now in Uzbekistan) in 1336. He was a member of the Turkic Barlas clan of Mongols. He first led a small nomad band to establish control of the area between the Jaxartes and Oxus rivers in his homeland. In the early 1380s, he invaded Moscow and stopped a Russian rebellion against the Mongol descendants of Genghis Khan. Eastern Persia fell to him by 1385, and by 1394 Fars, Iraq, Azerbaijan, Armenia, Mesopotamia, and Georgia were in his control. In 1398 he invaded India and sacked Delhi. He then invaded Syria and Asia Minor.

The Gur-e Amir is the mausoleum of the conqueror Timur Lenk, self-proclaimed restorer of the Mongol Empire. The mausoleum is located in the city of Samarkand, Uzbekistan.

He made preparations for the conquest of China but fell ill and died in 1405 before he could carry out his plans. Although his conquests were extensive, they were temporary and never matched the extent of the Mongol Empire under Kublai Khan. Timur's dynasty, known as the Timurid, survived for about another century. One of his descendants, Baber, founded the Mughal dynasty of India.

MING INVASIONS AND INTERNAL STRIFE

Ming incursions into Mongolia effectively ended Mongol unity. The Chinese were successful in penetrating deeply into Mongolia. In the Battle of Puir Nor in 1388, Chinese forces under the leadership of the Ming emperor invaded Mongolia and won a decisive victory, capturing 70,000 Mongols and destroying the capital city of Karakorum. The city was later partially rebuilt but was subsequently abandoned.

In the fifteenth and sixteenth centuries, Mongol supremacy passed from tribe to tribe. Military gains were made but never held, and politically all that was achieved was a loose confederation. First came the Oirat, a tribe of western Mongols, who penetrated into Tibet and Xinjiang, where the Ming were weak. Next the Ordos in the Huang He (Yellow River) region challenged the Oirat and warred successfully against the Ming. Finally, power came to the Chahar in the

The Hongwu emperor, the first ruler of China's Ming dynasty, is depicted in this fourteenth-century painting.

north, but tribal defections and the rise of the Manchu dynasty in China led to the end of the Mongol confederation under Ligdan, the Chahar leader, whose khanate lasted from 1603 until his death in 1634. This period also saw the widespread introduction of Tibetan Buddhism into Mongolia.

MONGOLS IN PERSIA

Hulegu, a grandson of Genghis Khan, set out to extend Mongol power into Islamic areas in the mid-thirteenth century. By 1258, he had captured Baghdad and all of Iran. He also captured Syria but was defeated in Egypt in 1260, after which he returned to Iran, where he settled. Hulegu's conquests resulted in the creation of the Il-Khanate dynasty of Persia. The Il-Khanate dynasty ruled in the Middle East from 1256 to 1335. "Il-khan" is Persian for "subordinate khan."

During the reign of the Il-Khan Mahmud Ghazan (reigned 1295–1304), the Il-Khanate lost all contact with the remaining Mongol chieftains of China. Mahmud Ghazan himself embraced Sunni Islam, and his reign was a period of Iranian cultural renaissance in which such scholars as Rashid al-Din flourished under his patronage.

Ghazan's brother Oljeitu (reigned 1304–16) converted to Shiite Islam in 1310. Oljeitu's conversion gave rise to great unrest, and civil war was imminent when he died in 1316. His son and

Baghdad, Iraq, is located along the Tigris River. This modern-day photo is a stark contrast to the way the city would have appeared in 1258, when it was captured by Hulegu, founder of the Il-Khanate dynasty.

successor, Abu Said (reigned 1317–35), reconverted to Sunni Islam and thus averted war. However, during Abu Said's reign, factional disputes and internal disturbances continued and became rampant. Abu Said died without leaving an heir, and with his death the unity of the dynasty was fractured. Thereafter various Il-Khanate princes ruled portions of the dynasty's former territory until 1353.

This map of the Manchu (or Qing) dynasty (1644–1911) indicates the boundary between modern China and Outer Mongolia. Under Manchu rule, the territory of China grew to three times its size under the preceding Ming dynasty (1368–1644).

THE MANCHU DIVIDE MONGOLIA

The Manchu finally conquered Mongolia in two stages that led to its division into Inner Mongolia and Outer Mongolia. In the late seventeenth century, the Manchu occupied southern and eastern Mongolia, which became Inner Mongolia. Though the western Mongolian Oirat attempted to unite the Mongols under their leadership against the Manchu, the eastern Mongolian Khalkha joined the Manchu in a savage campaign that resulted in the conquest of Outer Mongolia in 1759 and in the near extermination of the Oirat. The Manchu victory ended Mongol tribal warfare. It also caused the dispersal of many tribes into neighboring regions and the division of Mongolia into two political units.

GLOSSARY

administration The work involved in managing something; the application of executive duties; decision-making.

autonomous Having the right or power of self-government.

Black Death A pandemic that originated in China and Inner Asia and ravaged Europe in the mid-fourteenth century, taking a greater toll of life than any other known outbreak of disease up to that time.

bureaucracy A large group of people who are involved in running a government but who are not elected.

chancellery The position, court, or department of a secretary of a nobleman, prince, or king; the office of secretary of the court of a person high in authority.

clan A group of people tracing descent from a common ancestor.

confederate United in a league; allied.

councillor A member of a group of people appointed or elected to make laws or give advice; a member of a council.

khan A medieval sovereign of China and ruler over the Turkish, Tatar, and Mongol tribes.

nomad A member of a people who have no fixed residence but move from place to place, usually seasonally and within a well-defined territory.

pastoral Devoted to or based on livestock raising.

plateau A usually extensive land area having a relatively level surface raised sharply above adjacent land on at least one side.

revenue Money collected by a government (as through taxes).

Silk Road Ancient trade route, linking China with the West, that carried goods and ideas between the two great civilizations of Rome and China.

steppes A large, flat area of land with grass and very few trees, especially in eastern Europe and Asia.

subjugate To bring under control and governance as a subject; conquer.

subordinate Part of a lower class, rank, or position; inferior.

theoretical Existing only in theory; abstract or hypothetical.

tribal Part of or relating to a social group comprising numerous families, clans, or generations together.

FOR FURTHER READING

Burgan, Michael. *Empire of the Mongols* (Great Empires of the Past). Rev. ed. New York, NY: Chelsea House, 2009.

Byers, Ann. *The Golden Horde and the Rise of Moscow* (The Mongols). New York, NY: Rosen Publishing, 2017.

Dreier, David L. *The Yuan Dynasty* (The Mongols). New York, NY: Rosen Publishing, 2017.

Feeney, Kathy. *Marco Polo: Explorer of China* (Explorers!) Berkeley Heights, NJ: Enslow Publishers, 2004.

Goldberg, Enid A. *Genghis Khan: 13th-Century Mongolian Tyrant* (Wicked History). New York, NY: Franklin Watts, 2008.

Knight, P. V. *Genghis Khan: Fierce Mongolian Conqueror* (History's Most Murderous Villains). New York, NY: Gareth Stevens Publishing, 2017.

Kovacs, Vic. *The Culture of the Mongols* (Ancient Cultures and Civilizations). New York, NY: Rosen Publishing, 2017.

Lange, Brenda. *Genghis Khan* (Ancient World Leaders). Philadelphia, PA: Chelsea House Publishers, 2008.

Rice, Earle. *Empire in the East: The Story of Genghis Khan* (World Leaders). Greensboro, NC: Morgan Reynolds, 2005.

Shea, Therese. *Mongol Warriors* (Warriors Around the World). New York, NY: Rosen Publishing, 2017.

Whiting, Jim. *The Life and Times of Genghis Khan* (Biography from Ancient Civilizations). Hockessin, DE: Mitchell Lane Publishers, 2006.

WEBSITES

Because of the changing nature of internet links, Rosen Publishing has developed an online list of websites related to the subject of this book. This site is updated regularly. Please use this link to access this list:

http://www.rosenlinks.com/EIMA/Mongol

INDEX